FOR

I THINK YOU'D ENJOY THIS BOOK BECAUSE

FROM

PRINCIPLES FOR THE NEXT CENTURY OF WORK

Sense & Respond Press publishes short, beautiful, actionable books on topics related to innovation, digital transformation, product management, and design. Our readers are smart, busy, practical innovators. Our authors are experts working in the fields they write about.

The goal of every book in our series is to solve a real-world problem for our readers. Whether that be understanding a complex and emerging topic, or something as concrete (and difficult) as hiring innovation leaders, our books help working professionals get better at their jobs, quickly.

Jeff Gothelf & Josh Seiden

Series co-editors **Jeff Gothelf** and **Josh Seiden** wrote *Lean UX* (O'Reilly) and *Sense & Respond* (Harvard Business Review Press) together. They were co-founding principals of Neo Innovation (sold to Pivotal Labs) in New York City and helped build it into one of the most recognized brands in modern product strategy, development, and design. In 2017 they were short-listed for the Thinkers50 award for their contributions to innovation leadership. Learn more about Jeff and Josh at www.jeffgothelf.com and www.joshseiden.com.

The Government Fix
How to innovate in government
Hana Schank & Sara Hudson

The Invisible Leader (forthcoming)
Facilitation secrets for catalyzing change, cultivating innovation,
and commanding results
Elena Astilleros

What CEOs Need To Know About Design (forthcoming)
Using design to grow revenue and maximize strategic impact
Audrey Crane

To keep up with new releases or submit book ideas to the press
check out our website at www.senseandrespondpress.com

OUTCOMES OVER OUTPUT

Issued in print and electronic formats. 0911732
ISBN 978-1-0911732-6-2 (paperback)

Editor: Victoria Olsen
Designer: Mimi O Chun
Interior typesetting: Jennifer Blais

Published in the United States by Sense & Respond Press
www.senseandrespondpress.com

Printed and bound in the United States.
1 2 3 4   22 21 20 19

Joshua Seiden

OUTCOMES OVER OUTPUT

Why customer behavior is the key metric
for business success

SENSE &
RESPOND
PRESS

CHAPTER 1: WHAT ARE OUTCOMES?

In 2006, I was working on Wall Street for a brokerage that served the the largest institutional money managers in the world. Our system allowed their traders to buy and sell stocks on a massive scale; millions of shares of stock flowed through our system each day. Traders used our simple but powerful trading app to place their trades, and almost everything was perfect. There was one problem though: our business was built on a single type of trade. Although we were the best place in the world to make that kind of trade, we knew that if we were going to survive, we would need to diversify, to offer other trading styles to our customers.

Our founder and CEO, a visionary who had started two successful companies before starting this one, was confident he had the answer: replace our trading application with a new app—one that would support other trading styles. This new app would diversify the services we offered to traders, and protect the future of our business.

So the product team got to work: we designed and started building an ambitious new trading app. When it was done, it would be unparalleled in terms of look, feel, and function. But two years later, we still hadn't shipped anything. Leadership shut the program down. Despite the fantastic technical and design talent working diligently, the program had been a failure.

What went wrong? We had just spent two years making stuff. And we picked the wrong stuff to make. Sure, the design tested well and the prototypes looked good, but rest assured, it was the wrong stuff. It was too hard to make, there was no customer demand for it, and we could have solved the problem by making other, simpler things.

All that stuff that looked-good-in-planning led us to work for more than two years without delivering anything. We delivered no new capabilities to our customers, and we delivered no value to our business. Said another way, our team generated no outcomes.

If you've picked up this book, you're interested in this notion of outcomes, so let's start by defining the word in our context: **an outcome is a change in human behavior that drives business results**. Outcomes have nothing to do with making stuff—though they sometimes are created by making the right stuff. Instead, outcomes are the changes in customer, user, employee behavior that lead to good things for your company, your organization, or whomever is the focus of your work.

Looking back on my team on Wall Street, it's clear in retrospect that we could have managed the process and structured our project differently. We could have identified the outcomes that the business was seeking and found a much faster way to start delivering them. We could have done that by focusing on the outcomes that our customers—the traders—were seeking, and finding a way to deliver those sooner.

If this sounds to you like I'm saying we should have been more agile, you're right. That's what I'm saying. But here's the funny thing: that team was an "agile team." We had standups and stories and even an agile coach. We thought we were doing it right. But we were focused on the wrong thing: we were focused on what we were making—our output—which would be a big, beautiful app. We were building it piece by piece, and when it was ready, it would be beautiful, and then we would ship it to customers.

We should have been focused on something else: creating outcomes by changing customer behavior.

GETTING TO DONE: THE PROBLEM WITH FEATURES

It's common to get caught in this kind of confusion—mistaking "making stuff" for making progress, and mistaking shipping features for being done. It's a legacy of a time when we mostly made physical goods, and making stuff well was the primary challenge.

In the old days of engineering, setting project goals wasn't that hard. If you're building a bridge, for example, you know you're done when the bridge is built and people are crossing it safely. If you're making cars, you're done when they roll off the assembly line. But when you're making software products, done is less obvious. When is Microsoft Word done? When is Google done? Or Facebook? In reality, software systems are never done. We just decide to stop working on them, or work on one part of them over another. (And it turns out that lots of our work is like this—when is customer service done, for example?)

Even if our new software-based products are never done, why does that matter? Why not just make an endless list of features and ask our teams to work on that list—forever? In fact, a lot of contemporary project management turns out to work exactly this way. The problem with this approach is that features can be finished and delivered and "work perfectly" but still not deliver any value. Think about all those website pop ups that try to get you to subscribe to a company's mailing list. Do they work? Technically, they function as specified. But do they deliver value? Turns out that on the whole, they don't—people simply get annoyed and just abandon the web site instead.

Our world is full of "features" like this that work as specified and yet deliver no value—or worse, create problems we never intended. If you've ever used a microwave oven you've experienced this problem: how many of those buttons do you use in real life?

So if features don't automatically create value, then it follows that we shouldn't use them as the center of our planning process. In fact, we want to use a planning process that makes it possible to make as little stuff as possible and still achieve the outcome we seek. How do we do that? That is the question this book answers: we can instead use the idea of outcomes. Outcomes, or *the human behaviors that drive business results,* are what happen when you deliver the *right features.* **Ideally, they happen when you've delivered as few features as possible.** To get started, let's spend a moment to define some of our terms.

PROJECT GOALS: OUTPUT, OUTCOME, IMPACT

Imagine that you work for a charitable organization and you've been asked to build a well in a small village that lacks modern plumbing. You've been given funding by a foundation that wants to increase the standard of living in this village. They have observed that villagers spend a large amount of time every day walking to the river to carry water. The foundation believes that if the villagers had a well in the center of the village, they wouldn't have to carry water such long distances anymore, and they could use their time for other activities—ones that would allow them to improve their standard of living.

In the social impact sector it's common to use a model called the **Program Logic Model** to plan work like this and evaluate the results. In the diagram below you can see the building blocks of that model:

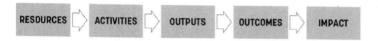

For our well project, the model might be something like this: we plan our **resources** (the people, materials, money, and other things we need), we undertake a set of **activities** (traveling to the village, acquiring and transporting our materials, building a well). If all of this goes according to plan, we create the **output**—the well. If the well works as planned, we achieve our **outcome**—people in the village spend less time carrying water. That in turn, becomes an important contributor to the **impact** we seek: a higher standard of living in the village.

Notice that the outcome—people spend less time carrying water—is a change in behavior that creates positive results.

Why do we need all these levels in our model? Although our ultimate target is to improve the standard of living in the village, that target is actually a result of many factors. To see if our work is actually making a difference, we need checkpoints that are smaller, measurable, and more closely connected to the work that we're doing. That's where outcomes are important. By setting our outcome as "villagers spend less time carrying water" we have an easier time assessing the quality of our work.

Outcomes for Managers and Executives

Setting goals as outcomes sounds simple, but it can be hard to do in practice. One thing that makes it hard is that we often set goals that are too high level—we tell a team to make our business more profitable, or to reduce risk, or something else that's really a factor of many variables. These impact-level targets are too complex to be useful to our teams. Instead, we need to ask our teams to work on outcomes—the smaller, more manageable targets that, taken together, will create the impact we want. We do this by asking them to focus on changing customer behavior in a way that drives business results.

We want our customers to log onto our site more often, or put an extra item in their shopping cart, or share an interesting article with a friend, or upload a picture, or complete a task in less time. What do all of these things have in common? They're all measures of customer behavior. They might be small changes in a big system, but they are specific, and they allow our teams the flexibility to figure out the most efficient way to solve the problem, to deliver the behavior change that we seek, and to make a meaningful contribution to the impacts (revenue, profitability) that our executive leaders care about.

So let's review: you can manage a team by telling them what to make: that's called managing outputs. It's a problem because features don't always deliver value. You can manage a team by asking them to target some high-level value, like growing revenue. That's called managing impact. It's a problem because it's not specific enough.

What you want is to manage with outcomes: ask teams to create a specific customer behavior that drives business results. That allows them to find the right solution, and keeps them focused on delivering value.

Early Value Delivery

The first Agile Principle says, "Our highest priority is to satisfy the customer through early and continuous delivery of valuable software."

As agile is applied to problems bigger than software development, many people who believe in agile principles have restated this principle. Today, it's fair to say: *our highest priority is to satisfy the customer through early and continuous delivery of value.*

Lots of companies that are struggling to get more agile know this. My team on Wall Street certainly did. And we believed it. It's one thing to know you *should* do that though. It's another thing to figure out *how* to do that.

It seems almost too obvious to say, but in order to deliver value early and often you have to have clarity about what "value" means. And it's a slippery term. As we move away from agile software to agile everything, we can't take it as a given that just delivering software is valuable. We can't take it as a given that just delivering any specific thing will create value. Instead, we need a more direct way to talk about value itself.

My team on Wall Street knew we should be delivering value sooner than we planned to—but we didn't know how to step back and think critically about our work. If we had known about outcomes, we might have been able to adjust course. We might have asked, "what is the outcome that our business seeks?" If an outcome is a change in customer behavior that drives business results, we could have asked, *"what is the customer behavior change that we are looking for?"*

We were looking for more customers placing new types of trades with us. It wouldn't have mattered if they did it in an app, by calling our brokers, or via their other trading tools. We were trying to diversify our business—building an app might have done that, but clearly, there were other ways we could have delivered value.

We could have asked, "why is it so important to build an app?" In retrospect, we wanted to keep our customer close to us, so we wanted them logging in to our software tools every day. Could we have imagined a software tool that took less than two years to build, but still got people to log in every day? Absolutely! There are so many tools we could have offered to traders that would have offered a small amount of value in exchange for a log-in. Trade monitors, market data feedback, performance analyses—the list is endless. But we never asked the question, so we never came up with these other answers—answers that would have allowed us to actually deliver value early and often. iteration

OUTCOMES, EXPERIMENTS, HYPOTHESES, AND MVPS

When you start thinking critically about value delivery instead of features, you very quickly run into a problem: how can we be sure that the stuff we're making is actually going to deliver value? For example, how do we know that the well in the middle of the village is actually going to raise the standard of living in the village? The simple answer is that you frequently can't know in advance. This is why, when working with outcomes, you need a companion tool: the experiment.

When you combine outcome-based targets with a process that's based on running experiments, you really start to unlock the power of agile approaches.

Think about the idea that a well would increase the standard of living. How could we test that? Maybe we could bring in a small gas-powered pump and some hoses, and pump water from the river to a central location in the village for a week. We could see then how people might use their extra time. Would it make a difference to their quality of life? Testing our ideas this way, before

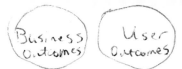

we commit to an expensive construction project is an effective way to manage uncertainty in our planning.

Think about my Wall Street team. How might we have used experiments? To begin, we could have asked, "what could we do to deliver value early?" A day or two of planning would have yielded many ideas, and many of them could have been tested in low-risk, safe-to-fail ways. And even a few small failures would have been better than the one giant two-year failure we experienced.

Combining experiments with outcomes is a really powerful way to work, especially in situations of high uncertainty. In these contexts, we're just not sure if the thing we make—like a new piece of software—is going to have the desired result for our business. Will our new trading app make our customers happier? Does it need to include all the whiz-bang features we envisioned, or could we do less work and release something different instead? How can we tell?

When teams are facing this kind of uncertainty, outcomes are a great way to set goals because they allow teams to experiment—to try different solutions—until they hit on the one that works.

And that, in turn, allows your team to be agile: you set a goal, design an experiment, then you test and learn, test and learn, test and learn, until eventually, you figure out the best solution. So you can think of agile projects as a series of hypotheses and experiments, all designed to achieve an outcome.

People sometimes ask me about the term *experiments*. Well, you've probably heard the phrase *MVP* or *Minimum Viable Product*, which the Lean Startup movement has made popular. There are a lot of meanings to this phrase, but the way I use it, it simply means "an experiment." An MVP is NOT version 1.0 of your product. Instead, think of MVP as the the smallest thing you can do or the smallest thing you can make to learn if your hypothesis is correct.

So, to sum up: an MVP is simply an experiment. Teams make MVPs to test an idea. They're testing their hypothesis about how to best achieve the goal—the outcome—they've been given. This is an ongoing cycle, and it's core to the agile approach.

When you plan work in this way—as a combination of outcome goals and experiments, you give yourself and your team the permission to go after a meaningful business goal, and you give people the freedom to experiment their way forward—even when the way forward is not clear. That's an incredibly powerful way to work.

Increment experiment

TAKEAWAYS FOR MANAGERS

» You can manage a team by telling them what to make: that's called managing outputs. It's a problem, because features don't always deliver value.

» You can manage a team by asking them to create some high-level value, like growing revenue. That's called managing impact. It's a problem because it's not specific enough.

» What you want is to manage with outcomes: ask teams to create a specific customer behavior that drives business results. That allows them to find the right solution, and keeps them focused on delivering value.

» For our purposes, an outcome is "a change in customer behavior that drives business results."

» Defining outcomes in terms of customer behaviors creates a more customer-centric and user-centric way of working.

» Outcomes and Agility: using outcomes to direct the work of your teams unlocks your team's creativity. They will work to find the best solution to the problem at hand in order to create the outcome you seek.

» To figure out if your outputs create the outcomes you seek, you need to test and run experiments. MVP is just a buzzword that means "experiment."

CHAPTER 2: USING OUTCOMES

The design guru Jared Spool asserts that there are only five things executives care about: increasing revenues, decreasing costs, increasing new business and market share, increasing revenue from existing customers, and increasing shareholder value.

Now, you can disagree with Spool's specifics while at the same time recognizing the core truth of the statement—that at the highest level of a business, leaders are concerned with the overall performance of the organization, and the performance numbers they watch tend to come down to these factors—which, in our language are high-level or "impact" metrics.

This presents us with a problem: when leaders want to increase revenue, for example, it's not as if they have a magic revenue crank that they can turn to pump out more revenue. (In the past, leaders might think about increasing production—making more stuff—but in a software-driven world, this particular crank no longer makes sense.) Instead, they need to work across their large, complex organizations to break down that desire for more revenue into something that the folks who are doing the work can act on. In other words, they've got to break down "increase revenue" into smaller, actionable parts. In the language of the Logic Model, they need to move from talking about impacts to talking about outcomes.

CREATING TEAM GOALS WITH OUTCOMES: GETTING SPECIFIC

Writing good outcomes starts by using the very specific, very narrow definition of the word that I shared with you in Chapter 1. For our purposes, we're going to be strict about this definition: an outcome is "a change in human behavior that drives business results."

The phrase "human behavior" can apply to users' behavior, customers' behavior, or staff and employee behavior—anyone who is part of the system can be the focus of this statement.

If we work inside an organization, the ultimate goal of our work is to help make our organizations more successful. In for-profit organizations, we're interested in things like revenue, profit, margin, costs, and loyalty. Those things are important, but you can see that they're not outcomes in the sense we've defined just now. Instead, they're impacts—the sum of a whole lot of outcomes. So we'll set those big impacts aside for now. We need to work on the component parts—the outcomes.

Finding the Right Outcomes

To find the right outcomes to work on, we start with a simple question: **"what are the customer behaviors that drive business results?"**

Let me give you an example of how this works. Let's say we operate an online t-shirt store, and we're losing business to a competitor. We want to work on customer loyalty, so we set a impact-level target—increase the rate at which customers visit our site from once a month to twice a month.

With that high-level impact defined, we can start looking at customer behaviors. We can ask: **"what are things that customers do that predict they'll visit our site?"** Maybe we know that they visit our site after they open our monthly newsletter announcing new shirts. Could we get them to open more new-shirt emails? That's a possible outcome: opening our newsletter more frequently.

Maybe we know that they visit our site after a friend shares an image of one of our shirts on social media. Could we get people to share images of our shirts more frequently? That's another possible outcome: sharing t-shirt images more frequently.

In both cases, we're focusing on what customers do— opening emails, sharing images—that predict the thing we care about: visiting our site. You'll notice something else: **because outcomes are things people do, they're both observable and measurable.** This is an incredibly important part of outcomes because it lets us use them as a management tool.

I hope you can see how this is both very specific, but also pretty simple to break down. You just need to remember two things: first, that an outcome is a human behavior that drives business results, and second, to figure them out, we just need to understand what our customers are doing that drives the results that we care about.

Leading vs. Lagging indicators

In our example above, we started to try to improve customer return rate by asking a question: **"what are things that customers do that predict they'll visit our site?"** The word *predict* is really important here, so let's talk about it for a moment.

One challenge is that customer return rate is a lagging indicator. It tells you how often your customers have visited you in the past, but it has limited predictive power. It can't tell you what you should do in order to increase the rate of customer visits. For that, you need to identify your leading indicators.

In the example above, if we can demonstrate that social sharing of t-shirt images increases return visit rate, then social sharing is a leading indicator. Knowing this, we'd want to do everything in our power to increase the rate of social sharing. Or maybe we can demonstrate that newsletter opens predict return visits. In this case, newsletter opens becomes a leading indicator. We can measure the rate at which people do this, and then we can start changing things in order to encourage this behavior.

These indicators have some important properties. First, they are measures of what people are doing—in other words, they measure behavior. Second, they predict the success that we're seeking. In other words, they're outcomes: **our indicators are the customer behaviors that drive the business results we're seeking.**

Hypotheses

Now you might feel a bit skeptical of the notion that either of our possible outcomes (social sharing or newsletter opens) will lead to repeat visits. It's possible that the t-shirt company in our story has data to support this, but it's also possible that we don't have that data—that the ideas are no more than hunches. And if they're just hunches, maybe we shouldn't waste time trying to get customers to share images of our shirts on social networks. Maybe we should spend our time in another way.

There's usually uncertainty when we're trying to generate outcomes. Will the output create the outcome? Will the outcome contribute to the impact? We often don't know—there's no data, or the data is inconclusive.

If we don't have the data to support our hunches, then we have to treat the ideas differently than if we know our ideas are true. We have to treat them as assumptions. The good news is that, thanks to the Lean Startup movement, we have a framework for handling assumptions. We can express our assumptions as part of an hypothesis, and we can run an experiment in order to test our hypothesis and see whether our assumptions are right or wrong.

A basic hypothesis has two parts: what we believe, and the evidence we're seeking to know if we're right or wrong. So, in our example, a simple hypothesis might look like this:

We believe that if people share pictures of our t-shirts at a greater rate, it will prompt existing customers to return to our site at a greater rate.

We'll know we're right when we see a correlation between social shares and return visits.

Experiments and MVPs

When you frame the problem this way, it almost begs for the next step to be an experiment or research project to see if your hypothesis is right or wrong. If you were looking at a statement like that in your business, you'd have to immediately ask: "what can we do to figure out of this hypothesis is true? **How do we know if we're right?"**

An easy first step would be to see if you have the data. And if you don't, your next step might be to run an experiment to see if you can observe a correlation. Earlier, I talked about the notion of MVP, or Minimum Viable Product. When I say MVP, this is what I mean: it's the smallest thing we can do or make to see if our hypothesis is true. And that's what hypotheses encourage us to do: to test our assumptions to see if we're right or wrong.

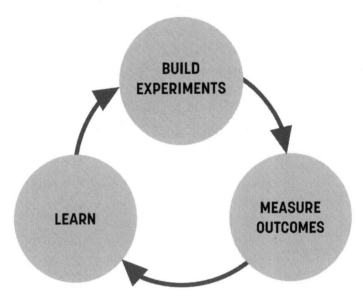

Outcomes are natural partners with hypotheses. When we state our goal as an outcome, we're either proposing some logical relationship between our work and the result we seek, or asking our teams to figure out that relationship—because we're asking them to figure out **how they might create that outcome.** And once we've proposed that relationship, we capture it in a hypothesis, and test it with an experiment.

The point here is that as we start looking at generating the outcomes we're seeking, it naturally drives us deeper into the dynamics and relationships in the systems we're designing, building, and operating. If we change this piece of the system, what happens? Can we get this result by changing that policy, this feature, or that marketing program? It encourages our teams to really dig in and get to know how our businesses really operate.

The Magic Questions

If you look back on what we've just covered, you'll see that there are a set of questions that we asked to help us use outcomes. These are really important. If you want to use outcomes in your work, these questions are fundamental. Early in my consulting career, I had a colleague who had a handful of very useful questions she turned to again and again. She called them magic questions, because they work like magic every time. These questions are my magic questions for finding outcomes.

1. What are the user and customer behaviors that drive business results? (This is the outcome that we're trying to create.)

2. How can we get people to do more of those behaviors? (These are the features, policy changes, promotions, etc that we'll do to try to create the outcomes.)

3. How do we know that we're right? (This uncovers the dynamics of the system, as well as the tests and metrics we'll use to measure our progress.)

Let's look at each of these questions in a bit more detail.

What are the customer and user behaviors that drive business results?

What's powerful about this question is that it changes the focus of your planning—instead of focusing on what you intend to make, you're setting your focus on the people you're trying to serve. It is a huge step to take if you're trying to make your business customer-centric.

Behind this question lie a set of related and incredibly important questions: What are our customers trying to do? How do they do that today? How can we make it easier for them to do that?

How can we get people to do more of these behaviors?

What's powerful about this question is that it orients your planning process away from features and towards behavior change. Sure, you might still think about features, but the goal of the features is no longer just to exist. Instead, the feature must be in the service of changing something. Making it easier for a customer to buy. Making it easier for a user to complete a task or achieve a goal. But this question also opens up non-feature possibilities. We might change policy, or pricing. We might change copy. We might change the way we position our product. We might change employee behavior when we interact with our customers. This question opens up our solution space to a much broader range of possibilities.

How do we know we're right?

Sometimes, we know there's a correlation between a user behavior and a business result. We might know, for example, that more customer visits to our e-commerce site result in more purchases. In this case, we'd be looking for ways to get them to visit more often, and the unknown here would be how we might get them to do that.

In other cases, we might not have any correlation at all. In the online t-shirt shop example above, we might guess that when people share pictures of our shirts on Instagram, then their followers are more likely to visit our site and purchase our t-shirts, but we don't have any data to support this hunch. In this case, we'd have to test a number of questions—can we get people to share pictures of our shirts on Instagram, and whether or not this leads to more visits, and in turn, more purchases.

Tracking Progress with Outcomes

Good leaders know to ask their teams to deliver value—in other words, don't just deliver *stuff*, instead, do something that creates value for the organization. But "value" is a tricky word—it's too vague to really get people aligned.

One consequence of this vagueness is that it makes it hard to track the progress of work. In my experience, this is because leaders and the folks who execute the work tend to think of value at different levels of specificity. Leaders think in high-level terms—appropriate to their level in the organization. Executors think in much more detailed terms—again, reflecting their POV from where they sit in the organization. In other words, leaders think about impacts, and executors are responsible for outputs and outcomes. The solution to this is to try to communicate in terms of outcomes AND the effect you want them to have on the impact the leader cares about.

For example, a leader may want to reduce cost. That's an impact. An execution team may understand that support costs are high because customers call tech support at a high rate. That's the outcome. They think they can reduce tech support calls by fixing confusing product features. That's the output. So in this case, a simple logic model would look like this:

» Impact: reduce costs
» Outcome: fewer people calling tech support
» Output: improved usability of confusing features

When leaders have teams that are working with well-defined outcomes, tracking progress becomes simpler—leaders and teams can review the hypotheses the teams are working on, they can review their progress towards the outcomes they're seeking, and they can look at a concrete measure: are people's behaviors changing? In this case, a team should be able to measure and report on the progress of their work simply by reporting on the rate of calls to tech support relative to the products that they're working on.

It's often the case that teams work on improving features based on an intuitive sense that it's the right thing to do—but this intuitive sense is hard to communicate, and rarely compelling to leaders. If instead teams can demonstrate through these models that their work goes directly towards creating a business impact that leaders care about, conversations become much more grounded, and teams and leaders become much more aligned.

Getting Started with Outcomes

Leaders who are looking to begin using outcomes to track the progress of major initiatives are often in a difficult situation. In most situations, initiatives are not planned in terms of outcomes. Instead, they're much more likely to be planned and tracked in terms of features built, or in terms of how they're tracking to some promised delivery date or other milestone.

For leaders in this situation, there's a simple question that they can use to start the conversation about outcomes: **"what (user/customer/employee) behaviors has this initiative created that are driving business results?"**

That question is the key to tracking progress because it moves the conversation away from features and reorients it towards value delivery.

For example, you might have a team working on an email marketing campaign. Email newsletters are an easy example because marketing teams are used to measuring their success in terms of what people do with their emails. Do they open them? Do they act on the calls to action? Are the actions that result valuable to the business?

But other initiatives tend not to have this culture of measurement. Internal technology initiatives are particularly bad. When teams are re-writing internal systems, for example, they often report progress in terms of how many system features they've completed. It would be better to instead measure progress in terms of new organizational behaviors created by their work. For example, what is the ratio of users of the new system vs. the old system? How many of those users are able to use a new business process as a result of the initiative? Are the new business processes unlocked by this initiative ones that in turn generate positive outcomes?

Technologists sometimes push back—they will make the claim that they can't cut users over from one system to another until the new system is complete. But this is where the power of outcomes shows up: no digital system is ever really complete, and conversely, even very small slices of a new digital system can start generating value before the rest of the system is ready.

So, if we insist that we measure value in terms of outcomes—how many new users are running through the new system—we can encourage teams to change their plans to deliver the outcomes we seek. Instead of planning for some mythical "feature-complete" future state (remember, software is never complete), they can plan to deliver value early, then enhance that value through continuous, incremental delivery.

This is how we can measure progress by using outcomes: insist that our teams plan in terms of outcomes, then ask repeatedly: "what new behaviors did your work create that are creating value for the business?"

Writing Better OKR with Outcomes

One planning system that's gained popularity recently is called OKR, which stands for Objectives and Key Results.

OKRs are popular because they help you connect your work to the big picture (the Objective) and they help make sure that you're not just making stuff or doing work for the sake of doing work. Instead, you're trying to achieve a Key Result.

But even though OKRs sound like a good idea, it can be hard to write good OKRs. One reason is that it can be hard to name the Key Result that you're looking to achieve. And when this happens, you often see teams just reverse engineering their current work into the language of OKR—which really defeats the purpose. The whole point of OKR is to help you think critically about what you're working on, not simply find a new way to talk about it.

So how do you write better OKRs? One way is to think of Key Results as outcomes. If you express your Key Result as a measurable customer behavior, you almost automatically have a well-written OKR.

For example, your objective might be to Successfully Launch our New Product. Your key results might be:

» 25 positive reviews in app store in first day
» 3 mentions on industry blogs before launch
» 1000 new user registrations in first week
» 25% of new users convert to repeat users

All of these are measures of user or customer or stakeholder behavior that result from your product launch effort. Now you'll notice that none of this is about what features your product has. It leaves open the "how." That gives you room to experiment with your tactics, but it aligns the team with the business result you're generating.

So, outcomes let you write better OKR by asking you to step back from your work, consider the meaningful business result that you're trying to achieve, and express all that in easy-to-measure terms of customer behavior.

TAKEAWAYS FOR MANAGERS

» Don't mistake impact—high-level aspirational goals—for outcomes. Impact is important, but it's too big for any one group to target.

» Use the magic questions to define outcomes: what are the human behaviors that drive business results? How can we get people to do more of these things? How will we know we're right?

» Remember that by "humans" we mean customers, users, employees, stakeholders, or anyone involved in the system that we're building.

» When you're planning work, be clear about your assumptions. Be prepared to test your assumptions by expressing work as hypotheses. Test your hypotheses continuously by working in small iterations, experimenting, and responding to the data and feedback you collect.

» Use outcomes to track progress. Leading indicators tell you that you're going to hit or miss your target. Lagging indicators show your target. Build an understanding of what behaviors *lead to* achieving the *targets* you seek.

» Use outcomes (not features) to plan initiatives. Ask "what new behaviors will this initiative create that will deliver business value? How can we deliver that value sooner?"

» OKRs can be improved if you think of the Key Result as an outcome.

CHAPTER 3: OUTCOMES-BASED PLANNING

So far, we've talked about outcomes as standalone targets. But teams often have to work with more than one outcome at a time. And leaders who need to coordinate the work of more than one team will also need to think in terms of systems of outcomes.

Understanding systems of outcomes and how they relate to one another is a big topic. In this chapter, I'll share with you one approach that I have found very helpful. (See the Reading List at the end of this book for pointers to other approaches.) It's a method that starts with a close look at what our customers, users, and employees are doing—their behaviors—and ends up with a roadmap, but a different kind of roadmap than we're used to seeing, an outcome-based roadmap.

Before we start though, it's worth spending a moment to talk about the complexity and uncertainty that we all have to confront when we work with systems of outcomes. It's tempting to think about outcomes as deterministic machines: I email customers. X% open the email, Y% click on the link, Z% end up at my website, etc. And while we may be able to track and predict those numbers, in point of fact, every step in this logical chain contains countless variables. The email has a subject, and body copy, and images. Which ones work best? What time of day should we send it? How attractive is the product we're offering? There are so many variables in this one simple example! And our working environments are rarely this simple.

All of this is to say that when we start to string together outcomes (if Team A does X, it will create Customer Outcome A, so Team B can do Y, which will result in Customer Outcome B) we have to be honest with ourselves about what we know and what we don't know. With that warning in mind, I encourage you to start working on your systems of outcomes by honestly assessing what you do know and what you don't know, then use observations of customer behavior, data about what people do, and experiments to expand the scope of what you actually know.

Roadmap to Nowhere

Few things cause more frustration in product organizations than roadmaps. Roadmaps—documents, plans, charts, walls of sticky notes—whatever form they take, are designed to create visibility into the future. Typically, roadmaps are nothing more than lists of features and projects that technology teams have promised to deliver someday. They usually cover the time period that stretches out from the current quarter and into the next year. And it's in this time period that the source of the frustration starts to emerge.

Roadmaps are supposed to help organizations manage uncertainty—they promise to answer questions like, *"what are we going to be working on? What are we going to deliver? When can we expect this new capability/feature/product?"* These are all reasonable questions. The problem is that most of the time, the answers that make it to the roadmap are guesses, fiction, or lies.

One solution to this problem: outcomes-based roadmaps.

The Root of the Problem: Output-based planning

Roadmaps fail when they present a picture of the future that is at odds with what we know about the future. If we were setting out to cross an uncharted desert—one that we cannot see from the air, and that was of unknown size—it would be crazy to predict that we could cross it in a few hours. How far are we traveling? What terrain will we encounter? What sources of food and water exist? You get the idea—you'd be reckless to make a prediction. Instead, you'd probably present your journey (if you chose to make it at all!) as an exploration. You'd ask backers for funding based on the tantalizing promise of what you might find as you explored this unknown land.

And certainly, if you had a map at all, it would probably showcase how little you knew about the terrain.

The parallel here for product organizations is that much of the work they plan to undertake has a similar quality: it's filled with uncertainty, unknowns, and perhaps unknowables. So promising your organization a plan that's filled with certainty is similar to promising an arrival date for crossing the desert. But that's exactly what we're doing when we build roadmaps around outputs. We're promising a certain feature by a certain date. And while there are cases where this makes sense, there are many more where, given the uncertainty, it's irresponsible to promise certainty (in the form of certain features and certain dates.)

A better solution: plan around outcomes

Instead of building plans around the outputs that you'll make, it often makes more sense to plan around themes of work, problems to solve, or outcomes to deliver. The less certain you are that your outputs (ie. the features you want to deliver) will deliver the results you seek, the more it makes sense to plan in terms of outcomes, and to build your roadmaps around sets of outcomes.

To do that, you have to identify not just a single outcome (for example, the way a team might identify a problem and work on that one problem for a while) but instead you have to find a set or a system of related outcomes that taken together will create the result that you want.

There are a number of ways to do that, but here I'm going to share one method that I've used successfully, and that can apply in a large number of contexts: planning a roadmap around a **customer journey**. You can also use methods like Impact Mapping, and Outcomes Mapping, (see Reading List at the end of this book) or any other method that allows you to break down big goals into component parts. But I really like using customer journeys as the center of the conversation, because we're trying to visualize human behaviors, and customer journey maps are designed for exactly this purpose.

Mapping The Customer Journey

A customer journey is an idea from the world of service design. It's a simple idea: you make a diagram that reads from left to right and describes what people are doing (their "journey") when they interact with your product or service.

So, for example, you might map a customer's experience when walking into a retail store. What do they see? What do they do? How do they find product, find help, pay, etc? This becomes more interesting when you realize that you can also map the journey of the other people who are delivering the service: for example, the staff in the store. What are they doing to deliver the service?

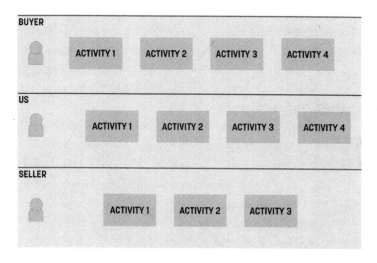

Building this diagram (sometimes called a "map") lets you and your team visualize what people **do** with your product or service. It lets you visualize **behavior**. This makes it very useful for finding outcomes, because, remember: outcomes are the **behaviors** that drive business results. So a customer journey map lets you see the behaviors in the system, which means that you can start to think about which behaviors you want to encourage, which behaviors you want to eliminate, and which ones might be missing.

Case Study: Improving NPS

Here's an example from a recent non-profit client. I was working
with a team that had been asked to raise the customer satisfaction
score of the service they delivered. The score they were using, called
Net Promoter Score or NPS, is used to assess the likelihood of a
customer recommending your product or service to others. The
team I was working with had been given a goal to improve their score
in the coming year. They were trying to figure out how to do this.

NPS is an impact. It's the sum of many factors. So we
needed to break that impact down into smaller parts: we needed to
identify the outcomes that would contribute to increased customer
satisfaction. Our first step was to try to understand the current
state of the service and see what was creating satisfaction today—
and conversely, what was creating dissatisfaction. We did this by
creating a customer journey map.

My client runs a two-sided marketplace. So we created our
map with three swim lanes: seller behaviors, buyer behaviors, and
organizations/system behaviors. Then, in each lane, we laid out an
end-to-end, step-by-step picture of the things people do as they
interact with the service and with each other.

This gave us our raw material: the behaviors of the people
and systems that make up the platform.

Next: Boosters and Blockers

With that mapped out (on a big wall, from left to right, with
sticky notes), we then went back through the map and asked our
magic question: *"What behaviors at each step predict success and
satisfaction? And what behaviors at each step predict failure and
dissatisfaction?"* We wrote the success factors (or boosters) on
green sticky-notes and we wrote the failure factors (or blockers) on
red stickies.

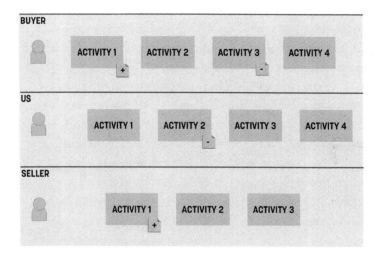

For example, the team knew that when buyers and sellers meet in person early in the deal, things go better throughout the process. So we marked that as important behavior to promote. The team also noticed that buyers and sellers had a hard time getting together in person because they were often located in different places.

With these insights, we were able to ask questions like *"how might we encourage buyers and sellers to meet in person earlier in the process? And, how might we eliminate the problem of location, which is causing buyers and sellers to get stuck?"*

Goals Transformed: A Roadmap of Questions and Hypotheses

And as we answered those questions, we started to come up with a list of things we wanted to work on. Instead of the vague (impact-level) request to increase NPS, instead we had a much more actionable set of things to work on: we want to increase the rate at which buyers and sellers meet early in the process. We want to decrease the rate at which buyers and sellers fail to meet due to problems of location.

Both of these goals are outcomes: they are very specific and measurable rates of behavior.

In this example, the team chose to stop there, and express the roadmap in terms of the questions we were trying to answer. ("How might we encourage buyers and sellers to meet early in the process?") We could have taken it one step further, and come up with a list of ideas for how we could encourage early meetings, and included those ideas in the roadmap. If you want to do that though, my recommendation is to avoid making a roadmap that's filled with answers and ideas. Instead, build the roadmap around hypotheses that link question and potential answer together. For example, you might say something like:

> We believe that if
> we increase the rate at which buyers and sellers meet early in the process,
> it will lead to more successful transactions (as measured by X) and
> higher user satisfaction (as measured by NPS.)
>
> We think we can increase the rate of early meetings [with this idea] and [with this idea] and [with this idea.]
>
> We will work on testing these ideas in Q1 of the coming year.

This Works for Any Impact You Seek

One final point here, you can use this method any time you're handed a target at the impact level. You're asked to increase sales? Create a customer journey map, and then review it with the magic question: "what are the behaviors in the system that predict higher sales, and how can we go about encouraging those behaviors?" You're asked to increase revenue? Same process: create a customer journey map, then ask "what are the behaviors that lead to higher revenue and how can we go about encouraging those?"

TAKEAWAYS FOR MANAGERS

» Planning with outputs limits teams' agility and problem-solving flexibility. Increase teams' capabilities here by planning around outcomes

» Create outcomes-based roadmaps that list questions, themes, and outcomes instead of features.

» One way to find outcomes is to create Customer Journey Maps. These maps help visualize how systems work in terms of customer (and employee) behavior, and so can help you find important outcomes in the system.

CHAPTER 4: ORGANIZING FOR OUTCOMES

One thing that makes it difficult to use outcomes inside larger organizations is that they're almost never organized around achieving outcomes. Instead they're organized around making stuff.

Think about how your teams are organized. Do you have a mobile app team? Or maybe two of them, one for Android and one for iOS? Let's say you work in a business that operates in an omni-channel context—a bank, or an airline, or some other business with multiple customer touch-points. How would the manager of an iOS mobile app team work on a broadly-defined initiative like re-engaging customers? Sure, she can do it within her limited scope, but wouldn't it be better to coordinate her team's activity with the folks running other customer touch-points? What about with the marketing team that's responsible for SMS and email outreach? What about the print advertising team that works on flyers and leave-behind promotions in retail stores?

In large organizations, coordination is always going to be hard—there's no perfect organization of course, you're always optimizing for one factor over another—but so often, our organizations are set up around product or channel vs. behavior or customer journey. And when we do that, we're implicitly de-prioritizing outcomes and prioritizing outputs.

It is possible to build an organization around outcomes though. In this chapter, we'll take a deep dive into one company that decided to reorganize their product team around outcomes.

HBR.org Adopts Outcomes

In 2016, the team at HBR.org decided that they needed to change. And the change they wanted to make was to move from outputs to outcome-based work. (I was pleased to discover that they got the idea by reading an advance copy of *Sense & Respond*, the book Jeff Gothelf and I published on HBR Press in 2017). They were generous enough (and brave enough) to share their story with me. It's a great illustration of both the benefits of working this way and the real-world challenges that teams face in adopting this system.

You probably know HBR.org. It's the web site of the prestigious *Harvard Business Review*. The site allows readers access to HBR articles, case studies, and other content. It's also an eCommerce site that allows readers to buy subscriptions, articles, books, and more. In 2016, the team had just finished redesigning and rebuilding what they call the "Item Detail Page" (IDP), a critical page for any e-commerce site. The IDP is the page that features a single product. It's where customers can see all the details about the product they're contemplating, and where the purchase decision is usually made. Getting this page right is critical to the life of an e-commerce business. And getting it wrong is costly.

The IDP project started when business stakeholders asked for a set of new features they felt would make the page better, and would better support the evolving business. The web team took up the work, yet the whole time they were working on the changes, Managing Director Eric Hellweg was quietly worried: "I realized that I couldn't confidently connect all those features to value delivered."

Eric had other worries as well. The team working on the site was small—there was always more work to do than there was capacity to do it. The team spent a lot of time managing priorities and negotiating stakeholder requests. It was tough to prioritize work. "Given the size of our backlog and our capacity issues, it was difficult to balance the projects we'd deemed important months before with the urgent requests crashing the queue," Hellweg told me. "We were feeling a growing sense of frustration."

The last straw was this: after the IDP project went live, the business didn't see the expected returns from all the changes. "There were lots of other factors in play as well—we went live in November before the U.S. election—but we couldn't help but feel that our resources could have been put towards more profitable areas," said Hellweg.

Around this time, the team started reading about the idea of managing by outcomes, and they started to reflect on the work they had just completed on the IDP.

The HBR team asked themselves, "How would we have handled this project differently in an outcome world?" Instead of focusing on executing against a requested list of feature enhancements to the page, they would have selected a few important outcomes and tried different approaches to achieve them. "I was talking with a developer after the IDP changes went live, says Eric. "He had a great thought—that instead of the project being called "IDP redesign" it could have been "Boost sales by 10% from IDP." Framed this way, the project might not have taken months. "Maybe we could have just made the buy button bigger!" said Eric, laughing. If that solved the problem, they could move on to the next outcome that was important to stakeholders. If not, they could continue to experiment until they have moved the numbers in the direction they wanted.

The more the team talked about the idea of working with outcomes, the more excited they became. Still, they knew that there was a lot to figure out. "We wanted to do it, but we realized that we'd have to change nearly everything," Eric told me. "The way we took work in, the way we prioritized, the way we executed on work and tracked the results."

Specifying the Outcomes

The team decided to try this new approach on their next big project. They wanted to reduce what they called "the subscription funnel bounce rate." This is the rate of people who click on the *subscribe* button but don't complete the purchase. Notice already the new framing: they weren't talking about features, but instead about generating business results.

The team used this reframing in the conversation with stakeholders. Rather than discussing a desired set of features to implement, they talked about business impact of reducing the bounce rate. Instead of getting opinions on what should be done, the team dove into the data to see where the bounces were happening, and then commissioned a number of user interviews with people who had bounced.

Looking at the data, the team discovered that most of the bounces happened when the price was revealed. Through the follow-up interviews they learned that the way the price was displayed was confusing. So the team worked to eliminate this confusion. They made the price appear on the first page, and added the functionality to simplify the price display by only showing prices relevant to the user's geographic region. "In the end, the project took some time, because of all the iterations and testing," said Hellweg. "But we were ok with that because we knew we were working on things that would definitely move the needle for the business."

In outcome-based work, teams need to be really clear about the value they are trying to create, and they do this by specifying two critical outcomes of the work: the outcome they are seeking for the customer or user, and the outcome they are seeking for the business. These two outcomes must be linked. In other words, you have to have a theory that if you create a certain outcome for the customer, this will result in a specific outcome for the business:

If we create *this outcome for the user*, it will deliver *this outcome for the business.*

With these two outcomes defined, teams can start to work on what combination of features, policies, services, etc. they can put in place to create the outcomes for the user, and thus create the linked outcome for the business. You might say, for example:

If we reduce the bounce rate (the rate at which users are frustrated and give up during the subscription checkout flow), *users will complete their purchases at a higher rate.*

Changing the Workflow to Support Collaboration

Up until this time, the HBR.org site had been managed by different product managers, each responsible for a different "place" on the site. Product Manager Jody Mak described the situation for product managers: "We each had our own little part of the site. I managed the article page, the home page, and some other places." Product managers didn't have their own dedicated teams, however. "This was challenging," Mak told me, "because we were each competing for [design and development] resources, and fighting for our own priorities." In practice, it meant that work was often delayed as product managers waited for people to free up.

After the IDP project, the team got together to reflect. Agile teams call this process a "retrospective," and it's a critical part of working towards outcomes because it gives the team an opportunity to learn what actually worked. The result in this case? "It definitely had its challenges," admitted Emily Neville-O'Neill, a senior Product Manager on the team. For one thing, the team was still struggling with problems created by their old, assembly-line style organization, that had them handing work along from design to development. That legacy organization isolates team members and slows down the process of finding problems. "We initially had trouble creating collaboration between developers and design," Emily said. They knew they wanted to keep pushing for earlier collaboration with the whole team. "We were fighting against waterfall design."

In the retrospective, "we workshopped a better design-to-dev workflow," Emily said. "A lot of it was about focusing more on wireframes and lo-fi design, both with users [during pre-release testing] and with developers. So we're making fewer assumptions and focusing more on early engagement between devs and designers."

This is a critical part of orienting your work around outcomes: if you're trying to figure out what is going to work for users, you need their early feedback in order to steer your progress, which in turn requires early collaboration across the whole team.

When Are We Done?

Another problem the team encountered was managing stakeholder expectations. One of the appeals of output-oriented approaches is that stakeholders like the concrete certainty of the plans. They like knowing what features teams are working on. Emily told me that the transition to this new way of working was challenging. "The business wasn't ready to pick a date and float the features," she said. "They wanted both a fixed date and fixed feature set."

This is common hurdle teams face as they move to outcome-oriented work. We're used to managing work with a combination of dates and feature specification. These are both concrete concepts, which makes them easy-to-use management tools: the deadline has either passed or hasn't. The feature is either finished or not. But as we've already said, there's a big difference between a finished feature and value delivery. When you're working on outcomes though, stakeholders still want to know when the work will be done. And they expect product teams to know the answer.

So how do you set expectations for stakeholders? When are we going to be done? When should we stop working on something?

It's hard to admit that the answer to this question can feel subjective: *we stop working on something when we've made enough progress to feel satisfied.* This means we have to define what result will satisfy us. Maybe we've agreed to working on increasing the subscription rate, *but by how much? When will we be satisfied?*

Well, that's a deep question, isn't it? It requires real conversation, real collaboration, and the maturity to accept fuzzy answers.

Eric offers another approach: "For us it's about establishing hypotheses and measures of success before we start on an effort," he says. "We get agreement on a direction for development and then commit to reviewing the performance for a series of months. If the change looks like it's working, we look for other areas of the business to work on. If it's not working like we thought it would, it raises the priority and we take another run at it."

Building Trust

To have these conversations successfully, people need to trust each other. And when the team shifted to using outcomes in March, 2017, trust between the team and stakeholders was shaky. One reason was that the team had a huge backlog of work, the pace of progress on that backlog was slow, and stakeholder frustration was high.

In the resource-constrained environment at HBR, stakeholders had to wait a long time for their requests to make it to the front of the work queue. As a result, stakeholders sometimes loaded up their requests for work, trying to get everything they needed into each request. This is an understandable approach when you have a limited window in which to get your requests serviced, but it means that the team doing the work has to service larger and larger requests. This creates a paradoxical effect: as the scope of each request grows, it takes teams longer and longer to finish each request. When this happens, the other stakeholders suffer even longer wait times. And so when their turn comes, they stuff their requests full to the brim too. This negative feedback loop will make delays longer and longer unless organizations can find a way to break the cycle.

At HBR.org, the team was seeing the real impact of this negative feedback loop: they had a huge backlog of work that they had previously agreed to, and every stakeholder in the business had his or her own backlog of work that they'd not yet been able to get into the queue. A review of the queue showed that there was *more than two years of work backed up*—it was 2016, and there were tickets waiting in the queue that had been submitted in 2014!

They needed to break the cycle.

Aligning Around Outcomes

They started by wiping the slate clean. They threw away their backlog of work. The whole thing.

Eric said, "We had been managing this huge queue of old work. We had all these old tickets. Hundreds of them. We got rid of all of them."

One stakeholder, Jeff Levy, Head of Consumer Marketing, recalls, "frankly, it wasn't going to get done anyway. We didn't lose anything except the false hope that it would get done."

The next thing that would have to change was the intake process for new work: how would the team work with stakeholders to scope and prioritize what to work on next?

For years, the feature-based way of planning work had made it hard to prioritize work. This is a basic problem of output-based planning. How can you figure out what features are important if you aren't sure which features will deliver value? The HBR.org team found itself in exactly this situation. Some tickets in the queue addressed the subscription purchase process. Others were about reading content. Some were hard to trace back to the problem they intended to solve. Emily described the situation: "we were comparing apples to oranges."

They wanted to work on the most important things first, and they knew that to do this, they'd need a way to align their work to business goals. That, in turn, meant clearly articulating these goals, both the longer-term strategic goals and the more urgent, near-term goals.

To do that they broke the year into quarters, and began holding goal-setting meetings with the executive leadership. The idea was to understand and agree on the top three outcomes executives wanted to get to in the next quarter. "We have annual goals," Hellweg said, "but we look at them each quarter to find the top three near-term goals."

After that, the product managers would share and discuss the Executive Goals for the quarter with functional stakeholders (marketing, sales, editorial, e-commerce, etc), then solicit their input regarding what to work on next. They asked stakeholders to make their initial requests for work by submitting tickets. A crucial difference this time was that they asked stakeholders to be more outcome-oriented. Instead of requesting features, "the ticket submission template asked for the problem, the hypotheses, baseline data, and what they hoped to achieve." Emily told me. "That made everything more problem-focused." In other words, they were asking stakeholders to think about the outcomes they wanted to create.

It turned out though that simply asking stakeholders to think about outcomes, while a step in the right direction, wasn't effective. Emily continued, "I would then go meet with the department heads as a group to prioritize the tickets. I remember that I initially asked them, "What do *you* think the priorities should be?'"

The result? "Some awkward conversations," Emily told me. "People weren't used to thinking that way for the whole business."

This is another normal stumbling point in these kinds of transitions. It's not just stakeholders who have trouble either. It's hard for everyone to shift their thinking from the concrete world of features to the abstract world of outcomes. It can help to do what Emily did next.

"In the next meeting, I asked them to talk about what they

were worried about. It was night and day. They started telling their stories about their business. The head of [one department] was stressed, because [critical metrics] were down year over year. All the other stakeholders heard the concern, and agreed, 'we have to focus on that.' It was the first time in the process that everyone was aligned," Emily said, "and it felt like a huge win."

In other words, by shifting the focus, the whole company was able to step back from feature conversations and consider the business problems they needed to solve—the outcomes they wanted to create. In doing so, prioritization suddenly became clear.

Organizing Around Outcomes

During this process, the team at HBR realized that if the queue of work was going to be managed in terms of outcomes, then they'd have to organize their whole group around outcomes as well. The team realized that they had two top-level impacts they were always working to create: they want users to consume more content from the site, and they want people to buy more things from them. So "buy" and "consume" became their high-level organizing ideas. Reflecting this idea, they created two outcome-focused teams, one for "buy" and the other for "consume." (Acknowledging the reality of operating a business on a day-to-day basis, they created a third "Operations" team to handle run-of-business work. For this run-of-business work, when you have high confidence that the solution will work, the outcome orientation is less useful and planning with outputs is often appropriate.)

Following meetings with stakeholders, the Buy Team took on their next mission: to improve a critical set of metrics in a particular part of the buying process. They worked on that project for eight weeks. "It wasn't enough time, but it felt good right away," Emily said, because the team made progress.

The initiative wasn't without problems though. Among

them, the critical stakeholder felt like she was being left out of the process. This is a common situation when stakeholders move from specifying outputs to managing outcomes. Outputs are concrete. You feel like you know what the team is going to work on when you agree on an output. Outcomes, on the other hand, are abstract—so you're just not sure what the team will be doing until you see the work in progress.

Jeff Levy, Director of Consumer Marketing for HBR, explained it to me this way: "it's a big fundamental shift, and it's giving up control. The challenge is that the people who are figuring out what to do are no longer the people who own the results. We're separating the responsibility. That's fine, but it's a shift in the way we think. The team can't go off and do this on their own. It requires a tight working relationship."

One concern for stakeholders is that they have a unique point of view. They are often the people with the broadest understanding of the way the different pieces of their business fit together. If the product team is just working on a single metric, they might improve that metric, but inadvertently hurt some other part of the business. For example, they might want to take something off a page to improve the clarity of the page, and thus improve conversion. But the thing they pull off the page might be important for another reason—a reason that's clear only to the business owner.

On the next project, the Buy Team focused on reducing the abandonment rate in the subscription, and as they did so, they were very deliberate about improving the way they worked with stakeholders. On this twelve-week project, the team increased the frequency of stakeholder check-ins, going from meeting every two weeks to having regular mid-point check-ins and being conscientious to create lots of informal check-points as well. "This time, we engaged our stakeholders better," Emily told me.

"They saw the benefits of this focus."

To build trust, the team also began sharing what they were learning in their retrospectives with stakeholders. Emily remembers one presentation she gave to stakeholders in which the majority of the presentation was an honest reflection on lessons learned. One stakeholder approached her afterwards and told her, "it's so refreshing to see the focus on what you learned. A year ago, no one would have stood up there and said, 'here's what we did wrong.'" Emily reflected on this experience, saying, "that's my one piece of advice: you have to be open to failing and learning and be open to talking about it."

Work in Progress

When I spoke with the team, they were about nine months into the transition to outcome focus. I asked some of the team to assess their progress. Kevin Newman, Senior Director of Technology, told me, "there's a lot of change, but we all understood that our old way of doing things wasn't working. Typically, change isn't a great thing, but this has been good."

When the team started making these changes, they also started measuring stakeholder satisfaction with monthly polls. "They were abysmal," Hellweg told me. But at nine months in, satisfaction was high. And, because the team is measuring outcomes, they're confident that their work is producing meaningful results for the business.

More than that, the new methods have produced a new understanding of the work that the team is doing. Kevin told me,

> as a media business, we had to shift our understanding of what a 'product' is—from being something that sits on a shelf to *organizing around an outcome*. To me,

that was a huge light bulb. I'd been looking for that idea my whole career. It is a way to organize people around something that isn't a discrete offering.... We don't have a product portfolio the way a product company would. But [outcomes] is a way to take advantage of the principles of agile that are all about producing value. It's great to see.

CHAPTER 5: OUTCOMES FOR TRANSFORMATION

So far, we've considered outcomes as a tool to help us create better products and services. The HBR. org story, for example, focused on that team's use of outcomes to improve their web site. And in Chapter 3, we saw how another organization used outcomes to improve a service they delivered—matching buyers and sellers on a two-sided marketplace. But outcomes are just as powerful when we apply them to the way we work—in other words, when we use them to transform our organizations.

The team at HBR.org had to **re-engineer the way that they worked** in order to implement outcomes in their work. They took an iterative and incremental approach: they liked the idea, so they tried it. After working in this new way, they paused for reflection, considered what went well and what didn't, and made some more changes to the way they worked. They were actively adjusting their own behaviors in order to deliver a great product, though they didn't think about or measure this behavior change in terms of outcomes.

The team at the non-profit team working on improving NPS took this approach even further. They used outcomes to change their own behavior. They examined and tried to change the behavior of the people who delivered the service (their own internal staff) in the same ways that they considered buyer and seller behavior. (When you're delivering a service, it's often easier to see the relationship between the way your employees work and the customer experience. That said, this relationship is real whether you're building products or delivering services—especially these days, as the line between product and service continues to blur.)

The point here is that you can apply the same thinking to the transformation of your organization—*how can we change employee behavior in a way that generates business results?*—that you use when setting goals for products. **Outcomes-based thinking is, in fact, the key to transformation.**

When you apply an outcomes-based approach to transformation I suggest you keep three rules in mind:

1. Your colleagues are your customers.
2. Everything is an outcome.
3. Everything is an experiment.

Your Colleagues Are Your Customers

I worked recently with a team charged with setting strategy for a particular region served by their global company. Organizational strategy for this region kept shifting. The strategy team felt frustrated—they complained that they were having trouble making progress because of the matrixed leadership structure in the region. Each leader had his or her own understanding of the strategy. "That's your challenge!" I told them.

According to Richard Rumelt, author of Good Strategy / Bad Strategy, "A good strategy is a coherent mix of policy and action designed to surmount a high-stakes challenge." One of the "high-stakes challenges" this team had to surmount had to do with aligning a fragmented leadership team.

Working together, we asked three questions:

» "What happens if we think of these leaders as our customers?"
» "What mix of policy and action could we put in place to get them aligned?"
» "What change in behavior on the part of the leaders could we observe to see if we've succeeded?"

Framed that way, the "customers" of the strategy were the leaders. They would "buy" the strategy or not based on how well it met their needs, the problems it solved for them, how well it was packaged and marketed, and the value it provided to them.

We sometimes think that customer-centric thinking is all about getting our external customers to consume our products and services. But that's too limited a view. In large organizations, where people operate very far from end-customers and end-users, we benefit when we use customer-centric approaches with our peers, colleagues, and stakeholders.

Everything Is an Outcome

When we're delivering products and services to external customers, we can observe their behavior to see if our work is achieving the desired outcomes. Are they coming in to our stores and visiting our website? Are they signing up for our mailing lists? Are they putting products in their shopping carts? Are they buying our product? But what does it look like when a leader in our organization buys our strategy? That was the next challenge our regional strategy team was facing.

I encouraged the team to talk about how the leaders were behaving today, and what new leadership behavior we were seeking. In other words, if we were successful in creating this new strategy, what would be different about leadership behavior?

"Well, for one thing, when you ask them what the strategy is today, everyone gives you a different answer. If we succeed, they'd all tell you the same thing—the same three bullet points," said one of the team. "And we'd stop reversing course every quarter," said another. "Right now, whoever argues the best in our quarterly meetings can change the strategy."

We continued that way for a while, and created a short list of new leadership behaviors we'd see if our strategy was successful. These included:

» When asked, leaders can recite our regional strategy as three succinct bullet points.
» Our strategy includes guidelines for changing strategy, and we observe our leaders using the guidelines in our strategy checkpoint meetings.

These leadership behaviors were (some of) the outcomes we were seeking as a result of our strategy. With these in mind, the next step was to actually define our strategy.

The behavior targets implied a great deal about what the strategy needed to include, and how it would be expressed. It would need to consist—at a high level anyway—of three easy to remember bullets. It would require some communication and internal marketing to create uptake among the leaders. It would need to include clear guidelines for changing strategy—ones that leaders could use in the difficult task of aligning and steering their organization.

Of course, leadership alignment wasn't the only challenge facing the strategy team. They had to deal with the bulk of what we normally consider strategy—what were the goals for the business in that region? What conditions and challenges did the business face? What policies and actions would they take in response? The team would be able to use an outcomes-centered approach there as well. But in any strategic effort, getting internal forces aligned around a shared understand is fundamental. This team chose to tackle that challenge directly by defining the alignment-related outcomes they would seek to create.

This is an important lesson for transformation leaders. When you are trying transform an organization, you are trying to change the way the organization works—in other words, you're trying to get your co-workers to change their behavior. Understanding your co-workers' points of view, their motivations, and the behavior change you seek to create is the foundation of any transformation effort. Expressing the change you seek in terms of outcomes allows you to build change programs that very specifically target the behaviors you want to promote.

Everything Is an Experiment

In the meantime, on the other side of the building, I listened as an innovation leader told me excitedly about the experiment she ran earlier in the week. She's been working on raising awareness for some important new technology inside the company. She wanted to see if she could communicate the importance of this technology and gauge people's response. So she sent an email to about 400 key employees, explaining the recent work of her team. The email ended with a simple call to action. *Reply to this email if you're interested in attending a training in this technology.* The response was tremendous. One out of three people who got the email replied yes—they wanted the training.

The innovation leader had behaved like a startup entrepreneur. Facing uncertainty about how to proceed on her initiative, she ran an experiment. She treated her target list of 400 employees as if they were her customers, then ran a small marketing campaign. She put her message out, gauged interest, and put herself in position to continue her campaign.

When you use outcomes to build your plans, you make progress towards your target by running experiments. We want to adopt a new technology? How would we do that? We might work backwards from the outcomes we seek: we want people to feel comfortable with the technology, so we want to offer training. We want to offer training, but we're not sure if there's interest. So we start by doing what the innovation leader did: run an experiment to address our first unknown (is there demand for training?) and observe the results. Did we create the outcome we are seeking? We did: people signed up for training.

Changing behavior inside an organization is a hard problem, and not one that is easily solved by planning on paper. Instead, it benefits from an action-oriented approach. You try something, see if it works, and if it does, you invest in the approach. This experimental approach to achieving behavior change creates a deeply agile way to approach transformation inside organizations.

TAKEAWAYS FOR MANAGERS

» When considering organizational change, take a customer-centric approach with your colleagues. What are their goals? What value can you offer to them in order to get them to "buy" the change you are selling?

» Frame organizational change initiatives in terms of outcomes. What are the new behaviors you want to create in the organization? What will people be doing differently when your change program is successful?

» Changing people's behavior is hard, and not easy to predict or plan on paper. Instead, take an action-oriented approach: experiment your way forward to make progress.

CONCLUSION

This little book tackles a big topic. That means that there's a tremendous amount of material that it doesn't cover. Some of that is by choice—you'll find further reading and resources in the Reading List, below. Some of that is because there's so much that I don't know myself. I've been using this approach for some years now, and I am still learning a great deal every day. Much of my learning has been guided by the people I work with and the people who engage with me to ask questions, teach me things that I don't know, and learn alongside me. If you'd like to do any of that with me, I'd love to hear from you. Email me at josh@joshuaseiden.com.

READING LIST

Methods for Identifying Outcomes

Gothelf, Jeff.
Outcomes Mapping
https://medium.com/@jboogie/execs-care-about-revenue-how
-do-we-get-them-to-care-about-outcomes-5d541a823358

Impact Mapping
A technique for identifying important outcomes. Note that Impact
Mapping uses the terms I've used in this book in a different way.
What I call an "impact," impact mapping calls a "goal." What I call
an "outcome," impact mapping calls an "impact." Once you're past
the different language sets, the Impact Mapping method is very
compatible with the ideas in this book.
www.impactmapping.org

Kellogg Foundation Logic Model
The language I use to describe outputs, outcomes, and impact
comes from this model.
https://www.wkkf.org/resource-directory/resource/2006/02
/wk-kellogg-foundation-logic-model-development-guide

North Star Metric
Another technique for articulating important outcomes.
https://amplitude.com/blog/2018/03/21/product-north-star-metric

Further Reading

Cheung, Marie. Outcome-based Service Mapping (2018)
https://blog.practicalservicedesign.com/outcome-based-service
-mapping-feec7e1937da

Fritz, Joanne. *How to talk about Nonprofit Impact from Inputs to Outcomes* (2019)
https://www.thebalancesmb.com/inputs-outputs-outcomes
-impact-what-s-the-difference-2502227

Fritz, Joanne. *How Nonprofits Can Measure Outcomes and Why They Should* (2018)
https://www.thebalancesmb.com/how-nonprofits-can-measure
-outcomes-and-why-they-should-2502307

Humble, Jez, Joanne Molesky, and Barry O'Reilly. *Lean Enterprise: How High Performance Organizations Innovate at Scale* (2015).

North, Dan. *Outcomes Over Features - The Fifth Agile Value* (2006).
https://dannorth.net/2006/10/28/outcomes-over-features-the
-fifth-agile-value/

Rex, Alice Newton. Outcome-driven roadmaps: A deeper dive into roadmaps based on outcomes (2018)
https://www.mindtheproduct.com/2018/10/escape-from-the
-feature-roadmap-to-outcome-driven-development/

Rumelt, Richard. *Good Strategy Bad Strategy. The Difference and Why It Matters* (2011).

Spool, Jared. Building A Winning UX Strategy (2014).
https://www.uie.com/wp-assets/transcripts/ux_strategy_means
_business.html

ACKNOWLEDGMENTS

A great many people offered help and support for this book, and I'm grateful to all of you. In particular, I'd like to thank people who read the manuscript, talked with me about the ideas in the book, and generously shared their stories. I'd like to thank the team at HBR.org, especially Eric Hellweg, Emily Neville-O'Neill, and Jody Mak who shared their stories with me. John Cutler, Dave Masters, Barry O'Reilly, and Misha Tepper all read the manuscript and provided valuable feedback. Alethea Hannemann and Rachel Swaner both generously shared their experience with Project Logic Models. Finally, thanks to Jeff Gothelf, who pestered me relentlessly to write this book. And finally to Vicky Olsen, my wife, my editor, my partner, thanks for all of that and more.

JOSH SEIDEN is a designer, author, and coach. He works with teams to create great products and services, and with leaders to help them build great organizations.

Currently the founder of Seiden Consulting, Josh was formerly the co-founder of Neo, the influential digital product innovation studio. Josh has also spent time on Wall Street, where he was head of product design at Liquidnet, the institutional brokerage firm. He got his start in Silicon Valley, where, among other things, he led pioneering interaction design teams at Cooper. He is a founder and past President of the Interaction Design Association.

Josh is a popular and highly sought-after speaker who appears at conferences around the world. He teaches workshops in Agile and Lean methods, and is currently developing training curricula in these methods for a variety of private clients and professional organizations.

He is an award winning author whose recent work has been recognized by Thinkers50 for outstanding work in the field of Innovation. He is the co-author of *Sense and Respond, How Successful Organizations Listen to Customers and Create New Products Continuously* from Harvard Business Press, as well as of *Lean UX: Applying Lean Principles to Improve User Experience*, available at http://www.leanuxbook.com.

Josh is also the co-founder of Sense & Respond Press, and is grateful to his editors there for continuing to put up with his nonsense.

🐦 @jseiden
💼 jseiden

Made in the USA
Middletown, DE
30 April 2021